MILLINERY HAT MAKING AND DESIGN

FLOWERS AND FEATHERS

British Library Cataloguing-in-Publication Data
A catalogue record for this book is available from the
British Library

CONTENTS

Millinery

Whereas 'hatmaking' is the manufacture of hats and headwear, 'millinery' also encompasses the *designing* and manufacture of hats. A milliner's store, predictably, is a shop which sells those goods. Historically, milliners, typically female shopkeepers, produced or imported an inventory of garments for men, women, and children, including hats, shirts, cloaks, shifts, caps, neckerchiefs, and undergarments, and sold these garments in their millinery shop. More recently, the term has evolved to refer specifically to someone who designs and makes hats, usually primarily for a female clientele. The origin of the term is likely the Middle English *milener*, an inhabitant of Milan or one who deals in items from this Italian city, known for its fashion and clothing.

Many styles of headgear have been popular through history and worn for different functions and events. They can be part of uniforms or worn to indicate social status. Styles include the top hat, hats worn as part of military uniforms, cowboy hat, and cocktail hat. Perhaps the most recent popular incarnation is the fascinator; a style which uses feathers, stylish materials, beads, pearls and crystals - ranging from extravagant to petite for brides, weddings, christenings, ladies' day at the horse races and many other glamorous occasions.

Notable Milliners include the German born Anna Ben-Yusuf (1845-1909), who wrote *The Art of Millinery* (1909), one of the first reference books on millinery technique. It was formatted as a series of lessons, each dealing with a particular aspect of constructing a hat, treating the fabric or creating different types of trimming. Ben-Yusuf also set up her own school of millinery, based in Boston and New York. On a more practical note, it also advised on correct storage, renovating fabrics, and the business side of millinery, and included a glossary of terms. Subsequently, milliners such as Lilly Daché have achieved notable success. This French designer made hats for many Hollywood films and movie stars, including Marlene Dietrich, Caroline Lombard and Loretta Young. Her major contributions to millinery were draped turbans, brimmed hats molded to the head, half hats, visored caps for war workers, coloured snoods, and romantic massed-flower shapes.

Today, designers such as Philip Treacy and Stephen Jones are at the forefront of the millinery profession. Jones especially is considered one of the world's most radical and important milliners, also one of the most prolific, having created hats for the catwalk shows of many leading couturiers and fashion designers, such as John Galliano at Dior and Vivienne Westwood. His work is known for its inventiveness and the high level of technical expertise with which he realises his ideas.

ARTIFICIAL FLOWERS

PLANTS AND FLOWERS

1. Artificial flowers, sometimes called simply artificials, were brought into prominence in the early part of the nineteenth century. The first ones were very crude, but wonderful improvements have been made within the past few years, and now flowers can be imitated with such lifelike and natural effect that one is almost tempted to search for their fragrance. Many materials are used for making artificial flowers. These materials are properly prepared by first being filled with a sizing, after which they are stretched on frames; and permitted to dry. This enables the proper forms to be cut out by the use of metal dies, after which the petals are shaped by being pressed in wooden or metal molds. Frequently this pressing is done at the same time the flower is cut with the dies. At the present time almost every known flower, grass, herb, and foliage is reproduced by manufacturers to be used as adornments for hats or for dress trimmings, and all these are included under the name of artificial flowers.

2. There is a certain kind of rubber cloth that is colored and used for making flowers, but this material is too heavy to be used extensively for millinery purposes. A certain kind of wood

which comes from China is bleached and specially prepared and then pressed into the form of flowers; but this wood is very brittle and the flowers break easily, and so it is of very little value so far as millinery is concerned. Artificial flowers are also made of leather, porcelain, and celluloid. Flowers are put up in bunches and sewed in boxes for convenience in shipping, but in almost all cases they should be taken apart and rearranged when used as garnitures for hats or bonnets. As all flowers, whether made of velvet, silk, satin, or muslin, are stiffened by sizing, they may be freshened by steaming with dry steam and then pressing the petals into proper shape between the thumb and forefinger. Flowers that are mussed can be made to look almost like new by this process.

3. Violets.—Violets, shown in Fig. 1, occupy a rather unique position in millinery. They are manufactured so that they can be sold for as little as 10 cents a bunch, while the larger double violets cost several dollars a bunch. The violet is a flower that is put on winter hats in the month of January in order to glide gradually into spring. In other words, when one has tired of the trimming on the winter hat, whether it be a hat of fur, velvet, or fur felt, the trimming can be removed, the hat steamed and cleaned, and then trimmed with one or two bunches of violets. Violets are also used to make a circle of flowers surrounding a white, pink, or deep-red rose. The violet is a flower that is extensively used in the early spring; but as summer advances it becomes the property of the woman

who has gray or white hair. Entire flower toques or turbans may be covered solidly with violets. When they are used as a foundation covering the hat should be trimmed with velvet ribbon or piece velvet made into a bow or an ornament. This velvet bow may be of light canary yellow, deep red, or a deep pink known as fuchsia or watermelon color; or it may be of black, white, and purple. If the brighter colors are used they should be placed at the back of the hat and away from the face, while the black, white, or purple may be used for the front trimming of the hat.

FIG. 1

4. Pansy.—The pansy, shown in Fig. 2, is made of velvet, but a cheaper grade is made of combinations of velvet and silk or satin. The pansy is more properly the flower belonging to the mature woman, and it is exceptionally elegant if used in the darkest blues or purple shades for blondes or women with gray or white hair. Entire toques or small hats can be made of these flowers sewed down flat on the frame, the petals of one flower slightly overlapping those of the next, so that the foundation is entirely covered. A hat made entirely of pansies and trimmed with either piece velvet or velvet ribbon can be worn by the mature woman in either winter or summer. Pansies are also particularly appropriate if used with the different kinds of fur trimming. They should never be used for children's hats, unless very tiny pansies are mixed with lilies of the valley or other field flowers that are especially used for children. As it is difficult to arrange pansies to stand high on a hat, they are used for the base trimming in connection with wings and aigrettes or ospreys. Small pansies are very good if used at the back of the bonnet for the elderly woman, and allowed to fall on the hair. There is no artificial flower which adds more life to a hat than the pansy.

FIG. 2

5. Forget-Me-Nots.—Velvet forget-me-nots, shown in Fig. 3, are the one kind of flower that properly belongs to the two childhood ages of woman. They are much used for tiny tots and also for women well along in years. When used for trimming hats for children up to the age of 5 years, they should be placed on leghorn hats or hats made of silk mull. They are extensively used for trimming bonnets for the elderly woman, particularly when they are produced in dark, rich colors. They are also used for making bands around hats. The flowers are separated and sewed down carefully to a rice net foundation that has previously been covered with silk to match the flowers or the color of the hat. Forget-me-nots are used for making the brims of close-fitting toques and for encircling the outer edges of cabochons, after which the centers are usually filled in with pink or red rosebuds. Care should always be observed to apply forget-me-nots to hats in the manner previously instructed, and not to use them indiscriminately.

FIG. 3

6. Fuchsia.—The fuchsia, shown in Fig. 4, is one of the rather heavy, rich flowers which should be worn on the hat of a woman of 30 years or over, and a woman of some size and weight. It is not intended as a light-weight garniture; therefore, it should not be used if an ethereal effect is desired. The leaves are rather large, strong, and pronounced, and as the flower itself is heavy in appearance, it is well adapted for the purposes described above. The fuchsia flowers may be separated and used for covering the brims of toques or turban shapes, in which case the petals must be spread apart and the flowers sewed down firmly to the brim of the hat. The same may be said of the use of this flower if it is intended to be used with others on the crown of a hat. If the fuchsia is used for a foundation covering, the trimming should consist of light-weight grasses, lace butterflies, or bows of lace or maline, in order to lighten the apparent heaviness of the fuchsias.

FIG. 4

7. Poppy.—The poppy, shown in Fig. 5, is most frequently made of fine, sheer silk, while the poppy buds are not infrequently taken from the natural plant, cured, and used in connection with the artificial flower. The poppy is most usually seen in its natural color of bright red and is frequently used for making an entire hat, not only for covering the foundation but for the garniture as well. If poppies are used for covering the frame, the petals are spread apart and sewed down so that the flowers will overlap one another. After the entire frame has been covered, poppies are clustered together in the form of a bouquet and used as a trimming. This kind of hat is strikingly becoming to blondes. Poppies are very much favored as a trimming for all-black hats of lace, net, and maline. Bright red velvet made into small bows and bands is the only material that assorts particularly well with the poppy. Poppies should not be worn by women who have flushed countenances or a great deal of color in their cheeks. In their natural color of bright red they are a little too warm for midsummer wear.

FIG. 5

8. Mignonette.—Mignonette, shown in Fig. 6, is invariably combined with other flowers. The mignonette of millinery has a function to perform similar to foliages that are used as borders for flower beds. It is particularly intended to enhance and bring out the beauty of other flowers. The mignonette shown in the illustration is frequently separated and each spray of flowers is used by being sewed to the edge of an upturned toque or turban brim or the edge of a hat. When used as a garniture the mignonette is invariably intermingled with one or more flowers of a different kind and color. The use of the flower in this manner is largely due to the fact that it is rather heavy in both weight and appearance.

FIG. 6

9. Dandelion. Dandelions, shown in Fig. 7, are artificial flowers that are usually made in the natural color. On account of the vividness of this color, dandelions should be toned down by being mixed with a quantity of grass or green foliage. They are exceptionally good for flower-trimmed hats worn in the spring, and are very good when used on all-white hats if three times as much green is used as yellow; in other words, two bunches of dandelions are quite sufficient for six bunches of foliage. The dandelion is one of the few flowers that are particularly good for a low, flat trimming, and when this flower is on the hat it should occupy the same position that it does when growing in the grass.

FIG. 7

10. Daisies.—Field daisies, or marguerites, shown in Fig. 8, should be used as garnitures principally on hats for little children, from the ages of 6 to 12 years. Daisies may be separated and sewed down so as to cover the entire crown, without having any green mixed in. The garniture should consist of a bouquet of daisies and foliage, and the flowers should be placed together so that they resemble a small hand bouquet. Life is added to the hat by adding black velvet or red velvet ribbon as a trimming, but the ribbon should be narrow and very little of it should be used. As stated before, the field daisy is intended for the little miss, and is not to be used for any other purpose.

FIG. 8

11. Grass.—The natural grass shown in Fig. 9 is packed in this form as a matter of convenience in shipping rather than for any other purpose. Small bunches of the grass should be taken apart and tied tightly to fine wires, after which the bunches should be intermingled with flowers and foliage. Grass is exceptionally good when used as a garniture to be worn in the months of June and July. If it is found that the dry grasses are inclined to shatter, they may be toughened by soaking them in alum water, as described later in connection with natural wheat.

FIG. 9

12. Enameled White Roses.—A cluster of wild roses with foliage of the same color is shown in Fig. 10. Both flowers and foliage, after being made, are covered with Japanese lacquer, which imparts a peculiar tint, so that the flowers and leaves take on the appearance of a piece of mother-of-pearl. Flowers of this sort are particularly well adapted for all-white hats and are considered more eccentric than the natural flowers. They are distinctly the property of the woman who is seeking something that is new and out of the ordinary, and should be used by one who dresses in rather extreme style or fashion.

FIG. 10

13. Yellow and Black Pond Lilies. Pond lilies and their accompanying leaves, shown in Fig. 11, are rather extreme and extraordinary forms of garniture that should be used on wide-brimmed hats. They are particularly effective if used as garnitures for hats that are made of nets and horsehair braids and are more appropriate if worn at lawn fêtes or afternoons in the parks.

FIG. 11

14. Gardenia.—The gardenia, shown in Fig. 12, comes in pure white only and is used as much in the winter as it is in the summer. The flower is clean-cut and should be sewed down firmly to the hat, almost as though it were appliquéd on. Gardenias show up to best advantage when they are trimmed on black velvet hats and used in connection with strips of skunk, stone marten, or beaver fur.

FIG. 12

15. Sweet William.—The sweet william, shown in Fig. 13, is made in many colors, but the bunches should be separated and intermingled with larger flowers and foliage. It is a flower that is especially well adapted to be made into long wreaths to encircle the crown of the hat or to lie flat on the brim. Rosebuds and foliage used in connection with the sweet william are the favorite combinations for making the wreath.

FIG. 13

16. Freak Rose.—The freak rose shown in Fig. 14 is a rather odd form of rose and foliage, not copied from nature, but intended to be used for trimming hats that require a distinctive ornament that will attract attention. Flowers of this kind show up exceptionally well on rather smooth, severe hats that are made of rich and elegant sheer materials. This flower should be attached to the hat upside down, or in some manner different from the way in which nature would present it.

FIG. 14

17. Sunflower.—The sunflower, shown in Fig. 15, is usually made of sateen, with a woolen center, and is obtainable principally in the natural yellow color. Flowers of this kind should be used as frame or side-crown trimmings, and as they are rather heavy, they must be placed on hats having firm foundations. Sunflowers are particularly good when mixed with foliage and used for trimming black or white hats with medium or wide brims. This size of flower should, under no circumstances, be used on small or dainty hats.

FIG. 15

18. Crushed Roses.—The crushed roses shown in Fig. 16 are made of silk or muslin, and in every color. Green, blue, gray, and tan crushed roses are quite as popular as those of the natural color. Crushed roses are separated and sewed flat so as to cover the crowns of hats, or they are used to cover the foundations of small hats or toques for all-flower hats, and are very extensively used for under-brim trimming and on bandeaux. Dress hats made of crushed roses are quite frequently of the same color as the costume. When crushed roses are used as a covering for the foundation, the trimming generally consists of an ornament made of lace or maline, a velvet ribbon bow, or a pair of man-made wings. Crushed roses may also be torn to pieces and an entire crown may be made of the petals of the flowers, the larger petals being used at the bottom and the smaller ones near the top of the crown.

FIG. 16

19. Rose.—The rose shown in Fig. 17 is made of muslin and is principally used for trimming wide-brimmed midsummer hats for young ladies of the age of eighteen or over. Several bunches are required for trimming the hat, and the flowers are separated and arranged artistically over the crown. Many people are under the impression that silk flowers are better than those made of muslin, but muslin flowers will wear longer, appear fresher, and imitate nature much more perfectly than those that are made of thin silk. The body of the muslin is sufficiently heavy to hold the dressing and the petals of the flower will not fray and become ragged as do those made of silk. In trimming a hat entirely with roses, extra foliage leaves should be added.

FIG. 17

20. Tea Roses.—The cluster of tea roses, buds, and foliage shown in Fig. 18 is used for bridesmaids' hats and for hats that are to be worn in June and July. These flowers should be separated and arranged rather carelessly on the hat. On account of the spreading petals of the tea rose, the flowers can be bunched together and made to serve as a base for a bunch of grass or other summery trimming. These flowers also assort well with fern leaves and are particularly well adapted for trimming horsehair, net, and lace hats.

FIG. 18

21. Flat Rose.—The flat rose and foliage shown in Fig. 19 are made of muslin and are principally used for trimming garden hats and hats that are worn through the middle of the summer. If roses of this size are used as a trimming for fur hats, or as a garniture with fur bands, the flower and foliage should be of velvet. If the flowers are used on a hat made of mousseline de soie, chiffon, lace, or silk, it is advisable to have the flowers of silk. Cotton or muslin roses are used on cotton nets and the cheaper and coarser braids.

FIG. 19

43

22. Ornament Flower.—The ornament flower shown in Fig. 20 consists of a cluster of petals glued to a flat foundation, with the four leaves so arranged that the flower takes on the general outline of an ornament. It is placed on the hat in the same manner as a buckle, a cabochon, or any other ornamental garniture. Flowers of this sort are used to cover seams or the joining of braids, as a finish for bands, or, in fact, for any portion of the unfinished hat that should be hidden or covered with the garniture.

FIG. 20

23. Lilac.—The lilac, shown in Fig. 21, is one of the most adaptable and useful of all the artificial flowers to be found on the market. It is one of the few flowers that are not made in this country to any great extent. It is also a flower that can be used as a covering for a solid foundation; or, as a garniture, it can be combined with pink or dark-red muslin roses and can be worn by young women, middle-aged women, and elderly women. Lilacs in white, lavender, or prune-colored shades are frequently used to make hats for the woman who has white hair. It is also the one flower that is largely used for going out of mourning. Hats that are intended for this purpose must have an equal proportion of black, white, and lavender. Lilac in its natural shade is the one flower that will permit the woman who has been dressing in deep mourning for some time gradually to emerge from somber dressing into one of brighter colors. Lilacs tied with black velvet ribbon and used on leghorn hats are much admired. Those made of velvet are frequently used to construct entire hats to be worn at evening functions during the winter.

FIG. 21   FIG. 22

24. Aster.—The aster, shown in Fig. 22, can be obtained in all colors, but it is most effective in pure white. The aster and the chrysanthemum in all white are the two flowers that are not suggestive of floral emblems. These two flowers, when used for gray hats, are greatly favored by brides, and the flowers are particularly effective when used as a trimming for tan, light yellow, and gray hats, and all hats of delicate pastel shades.

25. Dahlia.—The dahlia, shown in Fig. 23, is a rather prim and precise artificial flower that belongs in its natural colors to the blonde and the woman with gray or white hair. The natural shades of the dahlia are a purplish red; therefore, they are very rich and full of life so far as color is concerned. The flower in itself is rather heavy and is best used if sewed down flat to the hat. This flower, its buds, and its natural foliage are well adapted for making flower toques or turbans. The dahlia is a flower that can be clipped from the stem and can be used for making bands, one flower being sewed to the foundation directly in front of another until the band is of sufficient length. These bands are drawn around the crowns of hats and also used for the edges of wide-brimmed hats. The dahlia should never be used for trimming children's hats.

FIG. 23

26. Brown-Eyed Susan.—The brown-eyed Susan, shown in Fig. 24, is very similar to the field daisy, or marguerite, with the exception that in its natural state it has yellow petals and a very dark brown center. It is principally used for trimming black, tan, yellow, and pure white hats and is especially effective if wreathed around a hat for a brunette. Brown-eyed Susans may be mixed with white field daisies for the girl from 14 to 18 years of age, but they should not be used for young children, and they are entirely too gaudy for the middle-aged woman.

FIG. 24

27. Buttonhole Rose.—The boutonniere rose, or buttonhole rose, shown in Fig. 25, can be obtained in all colors and is used for corsage bouquets as well as for trimming hats. The single rose and buds, with a few leaves, are mounted on a rubber-wrapped stem and when used as trimming on a hat should be placed as though they were buttonhole bouquets. In other words, they are not joined together in a wreath or any other manner, but are usually placed one at the front, one at the back, and one at each side of the hat, with small flat bows of metallic, velvet, or satin ribbon placed between the bunches of flowers.

FIG. 25

28. Mock Orange.—The syringa, or mock orange, shown in Fig. 26, is made of white sheet wax. As the flowers are rather heavy, they should be mixed with dark-green delicate foliage or fern leaves. They also mix well with white foliage and white fern leaves. These flowers should be used for trimming hats for brides and bridesmaids. They are also good when mixed with black rose foliage and dark-red roses. On account of the weight of the flowers they should be trimmed on solid braid hats, and the frames of the hats should be sufficiently strong and firm to support them.

FIG. 26

29. Cornflower.—The cornflower, or bluet, shown in Fig. 27, is an artificial flower copied from the common field flower of this name. It usually comes in a bright indigo shade with a tinge of pink near the center of the flower. It is particularly artistic if intermingled with grass, foliage, wheat, field daisies, wild roses, and other wild flowers. It is one flower that is quite frequently used for trimming hats that are to be worn with costumes and dresses of all blue, either of the same or a harmonizing shade. The cornflower is particularly effective when used in connection with black lace hats, and also leghorn and all-white hats. It is appropriate as a garniture for hats for the young woman, the middle-aged woman, and the elderly woman. It is a good flower to be used on green hats, especially if it is mixed with dark-green foliage.

FIG. 27   FIG. 28   FIG. 29   FIG. 30   FIG. 31

30. Cowslip.—The cowslip, shown in Fig. 28, is a small, yellow artificial flower with a soft stem. Clusters of cowslips should be bunched together and rounded out in such a manner that they resemble the flower known as the snowball. They should then be sewed to the hat at the place where they are wrapped together so that the soft stems can be spread out underneath the flowers. Bunches of cowslips encircling the crown of a hat quite frequently have small velvet or feather butterflies in bright colors, poised on thin silk-covered lace wires, apparently hovering over them. The proper method of adjusting the butterflies over the flowers is to wrap a silk-covered lace wire around a darning needle four or five times in order to give the wire the form of a spiral spring, and then to push the end of the wire down through the flowers and fasten it to the hat. The object of the spiral spring is to keep the butterfly fluttering as though it were about to alight on the flowers.

31. Lily of the Valley.—The lily of the valley, shown in Fig. 29, is used to trim hats for the little miss between the ages of 3 and 5 years, and it is also extensively used for bonnets for the elderly woman. If these flowers are used for the young lady of 18 years or over, they should be combined with pansies or dark-red roses and green foliage.

32. Buttercup.—The buttercup, shown in Fig. 30, is of a dark, rich orange-yellow and is used with grass and wild

flowers on lace hats; but when used for the elderly woman it is one of the flowers that is quite frequently veiled with maline or lace of fine quality. Buttercups are quite frequently sewed onto a band in rows and used for trimming around the side crown of a hat. A ruffle of lace is permitted to fall over it, and the flowers peep out through and underneath the lace.

33. Straw-Flower.—The straw-flower, shown in Fig. 31, is a heavy flower principally used to trim garden hats or hats made of heavy straw braids. It is one of the few flowers not affected by dampness, and therefore it can be worn at lake, seashore, and other summer resorts.

34. Plush Rose.—The plush rose, shown in Fig. 32, is a flat rose made of rather long-nap plush. Flowers of this kind are especially well adapted to be used with fur bands and fur trimming. They are what might be termed more strictly winter flowers.

FIG. 32

35. Moss Rosebuds. Moss rosebuds, shown in Fig. 33, are very small rosebuds produced in many colors and are separated and used for making buckles, ornaments, buttons, and various other kinds of trimming used for misses' hats. The buds and long stems are sometimes plaited together in the same manner as braiding hair and used to rope around the crown of a hat, with a bunch of the roses hanging carelessly over the side of the hat.

FIG. 33

36. Cosmos.—The cosmos, shown in Fig. 34, is an artificial flower manufactured in all colors. It has a feathery center that gives the flower a light, airy effect, and is well adapted for what is known in millinery as banking purposes. The banking of flowers is done by grouping four or five flowers together and sewing them down to either the side crown or the brim of the hat, the flower itself being 11/2 or 2 in. from the point where the stem is attached to the hat; thus the flower presents a substantial appearance and yet is not held down tightly on the hat so as to destroy the apparent carelessness of arrangement it should possess.

FIG. 34

37. Chrysanthemum.—Chrysanthemums, shown in Fig. 35, are manufactured in many colors and may be used for covering turban brims and also for encircling the crowns of wide-brimmed hats. As the flower is rather heavy, it should be worn principally by the rather stout young woman of from 18 to 30 years of age. All-white chrysanthemums on tan, sand, or gray hats are particularly effective when worn with white frocks.

FIG. 35

38. Sweet Peas.—Sweet peas, shown in Fig. 36, are dainty flowers of many colors used for trimming hats for misses and young ladies. Occasionally, purple sweet peas are used on a turban or toque for an elderly woman; however, in such a case they should be used sparingly.

FIG. 36

39. Poinsettia.—The velvet-poinsettia, shown in Fig. 37, consists of a cluster of velvet leaves drawn to the center and finished with berries in yellow. Flowers of this kind are particularly good for trimming winter hats, especially when used with fur bands or marabou. They are also good on white hats for midsummer, particularly if the wearer has but little color in her cheeks.

FIG. 37

40. Orchid.—The orchid, shown in Fig. 38, is a large, aristocratic flower extensively used on lavender and all-white hats for young women, and also used on toques and bonnets for mature women. The larger sizes of orchids should be used for young women, while those on bonnets, toques, and turbans should be quite small. It is a flower that requires very little foliage.

FIG. 38

41. Dogwood.—Dogwood of all-white velvet with black stamens and black stem, as shown in Fig. 39, is a flower that can be used for either winter or summer. If used for summer it should be mixed with white fern leaves or white foliage, or white and black foliage mixed; but on winter hats it should be used in connection with rich velvet of a warm color, such as red, dark green, or various shades of purple.

FIG. 39

42. Wheat.—The bunch of wheat shown in Fig. 40 is made of silk muslin, the beard of the wheat being made from either hog bristles or goat bristles. Not only may wheat be made of artificial materials, but natural wheat is quite frequently used. If natural wheat is to be used, it is gathered 2 or 3 weeks before it is ripe enough to harvest. It is then laid aside in a dark, cool place and permitted to dry and cure thoroughly. When it is to be used to trim a hat, it should be soaked in a basin containing about 2 quarts of water in which three tablespoonfuls of alum has been dissolved. This solution has a tendency to toughen the wheat and prevent its shattering.

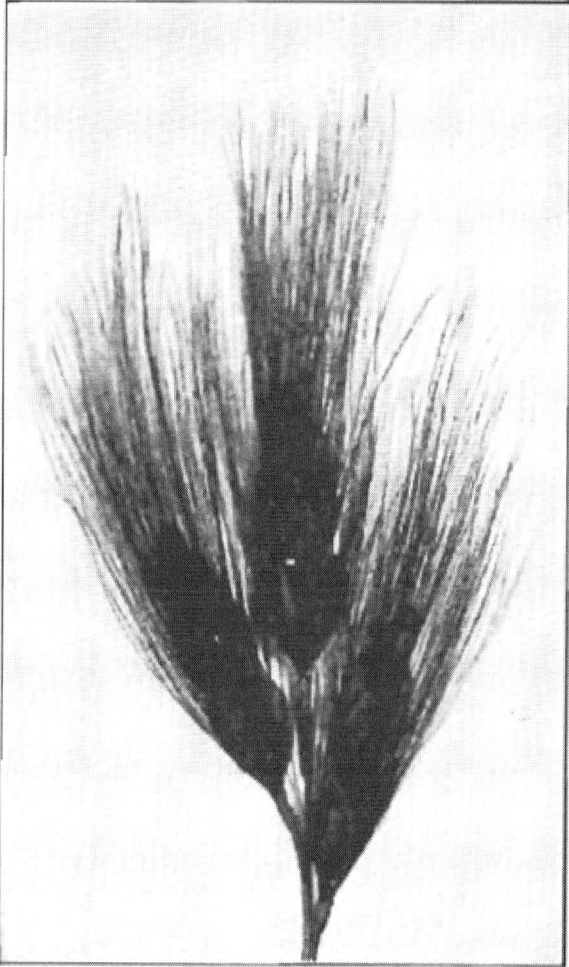

FIG. 40

43. Wheat combined with artificial buttercups, cornflowers, field daisies, and wild roses forms what is known as the Marie Antoinette combination, as these were used for trimming the wide-brimmed, high-crowned hats of the unfortunate Queen Marie Antoinette. This combination is used from time to time for trimming hats for young misses, especially garden hats or hats to be worn at afternoon lawn fêtes. Wheat in all black or pure white is much favored as a garniture for hats for elderly women. Wide-brimmed hats with dome crowns frequently have the entire crowns covered with wheat, and can be trimmed with field flowers or artificial butterflies. The field flowers should be wild roses, field daisies, and violets.

FOLIAGE

44. Many different varieties of foliage are imitated for millinery purposes; but, as many natural leaves are entirely too large to be imitated exactly, they are produced in miniature. When foliage is mussed it can be made as good as new by steaming and then carefully shaping each of the leaves between the thumb and the forefinger. If the foliage has lost its gloss, it should be brushed over lightly with shellac, using the same kind of shellac that is used for varnishing straw hats. If a dull, frosty appearance is to be given to foliage, it must be brushed over with a hair brush that has been dipped in melted paraffin. The paraffin hardens quickly and gives the foliage the appearance of being covered with frost. Rose foliage is so

closely imitated by manufacturers that some artificial leaves show worm-holes. All-foliage hats can be made by cutting the leaves from the wire stems and pasting them to a solid foundation, using milliner's glue.

45. Mistletoe.—The mistletoe foliage and buds, shown in Fig. 41, are used principally for trimming midsummer hats. It is a type of foliage that is well adapted for encircling the crown of a hat. When so used, it may be finished with a pair of wings or a man-made bird nestling in the leaves.

FIG. 41   FIG. 42

46. Aster Foliage.—The aster foliage, shown in Fig. 42, is

a very delicate spidery foliage that can be used for trimming lace or net hats. It is also used for covering white wire brims to make all-foliage brims, and it may be used for covering a wire crown for an all-foliage crown. It is particularly good for use with silk poppies or other delicate, light-weight all-silk flowers.

47. Baby Rose Foliage.—The very fine, small-leaf rose foliage shown in Fig. 43 is combined principally with small buds and used for trimming hats for misses between the ages of 6 and 10 years. It is exceptionally good if used with hats that have lace frills. A hat made with a careless lace ruffle drooping over the edge of the brim may have a wreath of baby rose foliage and buds encircling the crown and should be finished at each side with a rosette bow made of pale-pink or light-blue satin ribbon:

FIG. 43

48. Geranium Foliage.—The geranium foliage, shown in Fig. 44, is a heavy velvet foliage made in peculiar coloring. It is used over the crowns of dancing caps, evening hats, and elaborate dressy hats, and assorts well with flowers made of gold, silver, or other metallic materials.

FIG. 44

49. Lacquered Foliage.—The foliage shown in Fig. 45 is ordinary muslin foliage covered with Japanese lacquer. Foliage of this sort is frequently covered with a bronze lacquer to match bronze leather shoes. The leaves are principally used as a band around the side crown of the hat or for covering the entire crown of the hat, after which other flowers and foliage of different kinds are used as the garniture. The rose foliage shown in Fig. 46 is ordinary muslin foliage which has been covered with Japanese lacquer. As it is dark and heavy, and rich in color, it should be used in connection with roses that are dark and rich; for example, American beauties or the dark, purplish seven sister roses show up to the best advantage with leaves of this sort.

FIG. 45

FIG. 46

50. Lace Foliage.—The foliage shown in Fig. 47 is made in both velvet and muslin and is used as an eccentric novelty in connection with flowers that are of peculiar shapes and colors. The veins and the edges of the leaves are outlined, forming lace-like foliage.

FIG. 47

FRUIT

51. Grapes.—Both artificial fruits and vegetables are made by manufacturers for millinery trimmings. Grapes, cherries, currants, raspberries, gooseberries, and other small fruits are closely imitated, and if properly used make pretty and useful garnitures for hats. The grapes and foliage should be sewed down closely to the hat in order to imitate their natural position as nearly as possible. Grapes of the kind shown in Fig. 48 are used on winter hats as well as on summer hats, while those shown in Fig. 49 are of a smaller variety and are quite frequently used for making an entire fruit brim. As the grapes in the latter illustration are of transparent thin glass, the light shines through them and casts a pretty reflection on the face. If the grapes are spread evenly over a wide-brimmed hat, the wires should be wrapped with rubber tissue cut in strips 1/2 in. wide and 15 or 20 in. long, to imitate the stems of the grapes. The brim foundation is supposed to represent the arbor or trellis that supports the fruit. Bright-red currants or dull-green gooseberries can be used in the same manner.

FIG. 48

FIG. 49

52. Crab Apples.—The silk crab apples shown in Fig. 50 are rather heavy and therefore should be used sparingly on either large or small hats. They should be used on solidly constructed shapes, such as Milan and hemp hats.

FIG. 50

53. Gooseberries.—The gooseberries shown in Fig. 51 are manufactured in delicate green shades and are quite extensively used on black and white hats or various shades of brown. Fruit, as a rule, forms a more appropriate trimming for spring than for mid-summer hats.

FIG. 51

54. Cherries.—The cherries shown in Fig. 52 are manufactured in various shades of green, white, red, and black. On account of their weight, they can be used only in small clusters. A white hat trimmed in black velvet ribbon with cherries as a garniture is more or less popular every spring. The cherries shown in Fig. 53 are of a smaller variety and lighter in weight, and, consequently, more bunches can be used on a hat. This is the kind of cherry that is used principally for trimming bright-red hats, the red being relieved with green leaves. The combination of bright red and green is known as the golf combination.

FIG. 52

FIG. 53

55. Currants.—The currants shown in Fig. 54 are of bright-red glass and are used for making and trimming hats. A very popular way of using currants is to make a brim of green brace wire, using either sixteen or thirty-two support wires and double the usual number of brace wires. This makes a very solid brim foundation, similar to an arbor. Tie the wires together with green tie wire and then lay the currants on the brim and tie them in position with green tie wire. Spread foliage in an artistic manner and wrap the stems of the foliage and fruit with strips of rubber tissue 1/2 in. wide and 2 or 3

in. long. This wrapping goes over both the green wires and the ends of the stem. After the entire brim has been covered in this manner, a crown of braid or other fancy crown is used and the hat is finished with either a natural or a man-made bird placed at the side, as though the bird were about to eat the fruit.

FIG. 54

56. Blackberries.—The blackberries shown in Fig. 55 are principally used in small clusters on spring hats made of rather heavy braid.

FIG. 55

NATURAL AND MAN-MADE FEATHERS

OSTRICH FEATHERS AND PLUMES

57. Feathers of various kinds, especially those taken from the ostrich, have been used for trimming hats for more than three centuries. When they first came into use they were employed largely to adorn hats worn by men, but in the past century they have become the exclusive property of women, with the exception of those worn by certain military organizations and secret societies. A few hats for men, particularly the Alpine hat, introduced into this country from Switzerland and Austria, have one small feather placed in a bow at the side of the hat; but with these few exceptions feathers are used almost exclusively by women. Almost all of the ostrich feathers that are used at the present time are taken from the birds on ostrich farms, and are clipped twice a year. The feather is not pulled from the body, but is clipped off, and 5 or 6 weeks later the pin feathers are removed, after which the feathers grow in again and are ready to be clipped 6 months later.

58. The best and largest ostrich feathers and plumes come

from the male bird. Single feathers are only heavy enough to be used as ostrich quills or fancy ostrich trimming, while plumes must be lined in order to make them heavy enough for commercial purposes. The natural feathers come in various shades of gray and brown; thus, white feathers are made by bleaching natural feathers, and black feathers are made by dyeing. After the feathers have been bleached or dyed, they are starched and curled. The reason that ostrich feathers lose their curl is because the starch is affected by dampness; therefore, they should be kept in dry places and away from brick walls.

59. The ostrich plume shown in Fig. 56 is made of a single stem lined with three or four thicknesses of the feather in order to make it full and heavy. Plumes of this kind come in various lengths and all colors. The larger plumes are used principally on wide-brimmed hats, but occasionally a single large plume is used standing erect on a smaller shape. Ostrich feathers should never be used or worn with deep mourning; neither should they be used on hats for small children, as they are more properly suited to the woman past twenty. They should not be used on tailored hats, especially in the form of plumes; but, they are exceptionally good for dress and carriage hats.

FIG. 56

60. Prince of Wales feathers, shown in Fig. 57, consist of three small ostrich feathers, one placed high in the center and the other two placed just below, so that the flues of the two lowest feathers will cover the stem of the one at the top. They are frequently referred to as the Prince de Galles. The Prince of Wales tips are used for trimming hats for the mature woman and are quite frequently separated and used to encircle the crown of a wide-brimmed hat for a younger woman. In case they are used in this manner the wire stems should be cut off and the back of the feather sewed firmly to the hat. Small feathers that are attached to the side crown of the hat should be sewed on with silk floss matching the feather in color. Sew over the stem but not through it, so that, after the entire hat is trimmed, each feather may be twisted and turned to its proper position.

FIG. 57

61. In case a feather is not bent properly, the stem can be creased and bent backwards, forwards, or sidewise, so that the feather will take on the outline of the crown or fit closely and snugly to the hat. This is done by holding the feather curler in the hand with the curved edge of the blade up, placing the stem of the feather directly over it, and pressing the feather down onto the knife with the thumb. The indentation made by the knife on the side of the stem permits the stem to be bent backwards or forwards as desired. Feathers can be bent over the blade of an ordinary table knife if a curling knife is not at hand. If a long ostrich plume is bent over a knife so that the feather may be used to encircle the crown of a hat with the under side of the feather showing to the front, the plume or feather is then known as a *lobster feather*. When a long ostrich plume has the flues curled in such a manner that the stem is entirely hidden, it is known as an *Amazon plume*. Large plumes are used for trimming Gainsborough hats. Small women should not wear large plumes, as they are out of proportion to the weight of the body and the general build of the person.

62. The ostrich fancy plume shown in Fig. 58 is made of several quills of uncurled ostrich, used one on top of the other, the stem of the ostrich quill being covered with hackle feathers which are pasted onto the stem of the ostrich feather. Feathers of this sort are used principally for trimming medium-sized or large hats, used for restaurant, carriage, or evening wear.

100

FIG. 58

63. Uncurled ostrich was introduced to the fashionable woman by an accident. Many well-dressed women attended a race meet in Paris and were drenched by a shower, which removed the curl from the ostrich feathers they wore; but as the appearance of the uncurled ostrich was rather pleasing to the eye, the next day the demand for uncurled ostrich was created, and it has been more or less popular ever since.

64. The ostrich fancy quill shown in Fig. 59 is made by soaking the central portion of the feather in acid so as to remove some of the flues. The ends of the feathers are not soaked; consequently, they retain their natural form. This feather is shown in a single quill, the base of which is finished with a fancy ball made of ostrich flues and an ostrich pompon. Fancy feathers of this kind are used principally on the dressier hats; but occasionally a quill of this kind is used on a very handsome street hat, especially if the hat is made of rich velvet or long-pile plush.

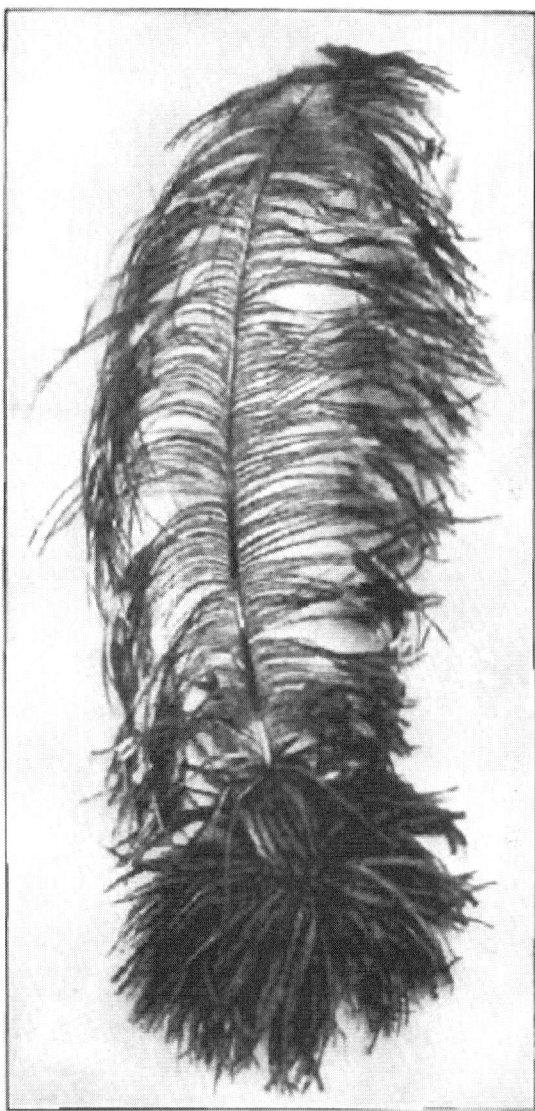

FIG. 59

65. The curled ostrich quill shown in Fig. 60 consists of a single quill having only the ends of the flues curled on the curling knife. Feathers of this sort are used principally for high trimming, but sometimes as many as ten or twelve are used on one hat, entirely encircling the crown and standing high in the air, all of the points of the feathers coming close together at the center. This arrangement of the trimming resembles the head-dress of an Indian chief. Only the best feathers can be used for this purpose. Quite frequently two or three ostrich quills are placed erect in the air on the side of a small hat that is worn with a tailored costume.

FIG. 60

66. The double fancy plume shown in Fig. 61 is made of two quills of ostrich fastened together, back to back, and tied firmly together at the bottom and at a point 6 or 7 in. from the bottom. The tips of the feathers are curled over as shown in the illustration, while the flues at the bottom of the feather remain straight. Fancy ostrich feathers of this kind are used principally on the dressier hats.

FIG. 61

67. Very small single-quill ostrich feathers may have the flues and ends turned down to the bottom and tied firmly together, thus forming the trimming known as ostrich-egg trimming. This arrangement of the feather is shown in Fig. 62. Five or six such feathers are usually clustered together in one bunch when used as a garniture; or, they may be separated and used to encircle the crown of the hat. The wrapping at the bottom of the ostrich-egg trimming must always be covered. Chenille cords of the same color as the feather make a beautiful finish for garnitures of this sort.

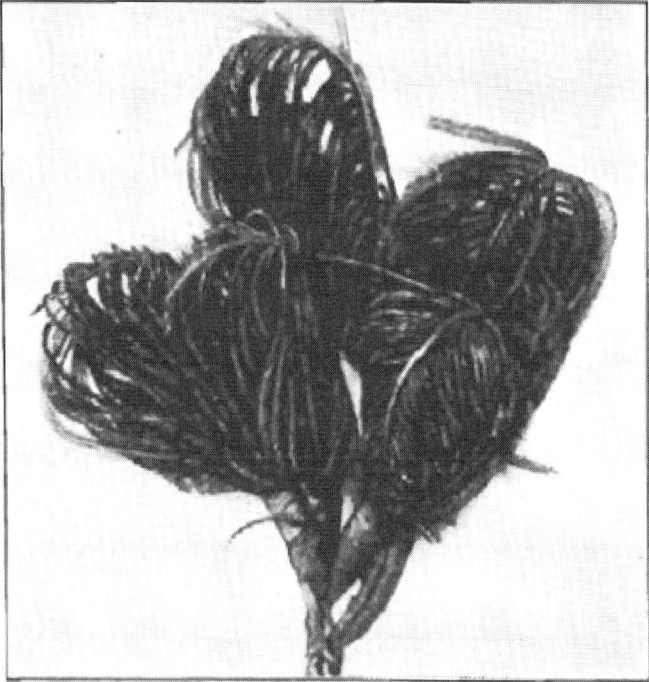

FIG. 62

68. The ostrich feather band, shown in Fig. 63, is made of single feathers sewed together, one overlapping the end of the other, so as to make long strips. These bands have the flues on both sides curled in and are used for the edges of hats, for bands around small hats for mature women, and also for covering the entire frame or foundation for bonnets for the elderly woman. Wire frames covered with maline are sometimes entirely covered with ostrich bands in order to make an ostrich hat. Ostrich bands are quite frequently used for trimming evening wraps, dresses, muffs, and scarfs.

FIG. 63

WINGS

69. On account of the strong efforts of different societies and clubs that are working to prevent the extermination of both native and foreign birds, manufacturers of millinery within the last few years have placed on the market what are known as man-made birds and wings. These wings and birds are made on net foundations that are wired so that they can be bent into various forms and shapes. They are a great improvement over natural wings, because the feathers that are used in almost all cases are taken from fowls that are used for food, such as the chicken, duck, goose, turkey, pheasant, prairie hen, guinea hen, pigeon, and others, and the manufacturer is at liberty to use the feathers of any fowl or bird that is killed for food, without interference by law; also, the man-made bird or wing contains no bones or pieces of flesh, and therefore they are more sanitary.

70. Man-made wings are either glued or sewed together, fish glue being used to stick the feathers to the net foundation. Should such wings come apart, they can be stuck together again by using milliner's glue. It is not an uncommon thing to cover wings with one thickness of maline, but this should be avoided if possible. A wing that is sewed to the hat should

be fastened with the stab-stitch; but the thread should not be drawn too tight, or it will show in the wing where the stitches are made. The wired end of the wing may be stuck through the top crown or the side crown and fastened on the inside of the hat, which will later be covered with a lining. The end of the wire must be turned back and sewed down close to the hat, so as not to catch in the hair.

71. The large wing shown in Fig. 64 is made of wing feathers finished with hackle feathers at the bottom. Hackle feathers are obtained from the neck of the rooster and are soft, so that a wing of this kind can be bent to fit the form of the hat. Large wings of this kind are invariably used on large hats; but if they are to be used on smaller hats they are curled in on both outer edges so that the wing will stand erect. Wings of this kind are principally used for tailored or semi-tailored hats.

FIG. 64

72. The small wing shown in Fig. 65 is a man-made wing in the shape of two fans joined together at the bottom and ornamented with glass beads fastened on wires that run through the center of the wing. Wings of this kind are used where a low crown trimming is desired. They are particularly effective if a half dozen of them are fastened around the side crown of the hat, spaced at equal distances, with the fans spread out on the brim. Another pretty arrangement is to have a wreath of flowers and foliage entirely encircling the hat and to use one of these wings nestling in the flowers at each side of the hat. Wings of this kind may also be used on bonnets for elderly women.

FIG. 65

73. In Fig. 66 is shown a pair of small specially shaped man-made wings, constructed on a net foundation. Wings of this kind are used on hats in about the same manner in which a butterfly would be attached as a trimming; that is, they are sewed in the center of a round, small wreath of flowers. They may also be separated and sewed flat to the crown, to make an all-feather hat, the tip of one wing overlapping the base of the next. These wings can also be attached to the wide brim of a hat. When so used, they should be placed on the brim about half way between the outer edge of the hat and the head-size, and should stand erect on the brim, resembling a butterfly with folded wings that has just alighted on a flower.

FIG. 66

74. The pair of wings shown in Fig. 67 are man-made wings, known as left and right, and are of different forms. The larger wing may stand erect in the air at the side of a hat while the smaller wing may be used to curve around and cover the base of the first wing. Wings of this kind can be twisted and bent and placed on hats in various eccentric and artistic forms, but great care must be exercised to maintain the general outline of the hat; that is, they should not be too heavy at one side nor hang off the hat so as to appear to throw the hat out of balance.

FIG. 67

75. The wing shown in Fig. 68 is made of wing feathers combined with hackle feathers and usually comes in pairs. Such wings are quite strong in construction and can be used advantageously to add height to a hat. Four of them can be placed on the apex of the crown of a hat and may stand erect in the air; or both of them may be used at one side; or two pairs of the wings may be spread out and laid flat on top of the crown so that the points of the wings will project evenly at each side. This produces a wide, effective trimming that is very becoming to certain types of women.

FIG. 68

76. The wing shown in Fig. 69 is a top-knot wing that can be used for many purposes. As wings of this kind come in pairs, several of them may be separated and used around a hat, the wing part of the top being curved so that the row will entirely encircle the crown. They may also be sewed flat on a turban brim in order to make a feather band for the hat. One pair of these wings may be used for trimming a small turban for the slender woman and the same kind of wing may be used on a bonnet or toque for the elderly woman.

FIG. 69

77. The wings shown in Fig. 70 are known as Alsatian wings. They are man-made, soft, and pliable, and have the general form and outline of an Alsatian bow. A pair of wings of this kind can be spread apart and used on a wide-brimmed hat, or they may be closed together so that they are back to back and used on a smaller hat. The feather ornament at the center is pressed down close to the hat to cover the wire stem at the end of each wing. These wings have had the quill of each feather pared or scraped off so that the feather is soft; therefore, it does not blow away easily.

FIG. 70

78. The wings shown in Fig. 71 are man-made wings, not copied from Nature, but are frequently referred to as angel's wings or Mercury wings. They may be sewed down flat on the brim of a wide-brimmed hat or they may stand erect in the air. They may be folded together so that they are back to back and placed on each side of a turban or small hat, and can also be used on bonnets for elderly women.

FIG. 71

79. The wing shown in Fig. 72 is a large wing made from the wing feathers of the goose, some of the wing feathers of the mallard duck, and the breast feathers of the pheasant. Wings of this kind are intended to stand high on the hat, and being of a rather eccentric form they can be bent and adjusted in numerous ways. They may be folded together near the center at the bottom and placed on a wide-brimmed hat to extend out on both sides of the hat. If this is done, two wings will be required, one for the left side and one for the right side of the hat.

FIG. 72

80. The small wing made of hackle feathers, shown in Fig. 73, may be used for covering the crown of a hat, may be sewed flat on the brim to make an all-feather brim, or it may be used for trimming a small turban or bonnet for an elderly woman. When used for the latter purpose, two wings should be used, and they should stand erect in the center of the bonnet. These feathers are light and very soft and fluffy, and are admirably adapted for use on all hats that must be light in weight.

FIG. 73

81. Preserving Wings.—Should one desire to use the wings of the duck or the pheasant, or the wing of any other bird, with the bone remaining in the wing, powdered arsenic must be well rubbed into the feathers and the bone in order to kill insects and prevent the wing from being damaged by moths. As arsenic is a poison, it must be handled with great care. Lay the wing on a table so that the inside is face up. With a sharp-pointed knife, as shown in Fig. 74, cut in to the bone and with the pointed end of the knife scrape away all the flesh. After this has been done, rub powdered arsenic in and around the bone and all through the feathers to prevent moths from eating the wing. The easiest method of applying the arsenic is to put some of it in a tin pepper-box or a talcum-powder box that has small perforated openings at the top. Shake the box and the powder will fall lightly on the feathers of the wing. After the wing has been thus treated, it should be placed under books or a weight to flatten it out and preserve its shape. Should the wing be very large, the bone may be broken into bits by striking the wing with a hammer or hatchet, after which the small pieces can readily be removed. Large wings must be wired if they are intended to stand erect on a hat.

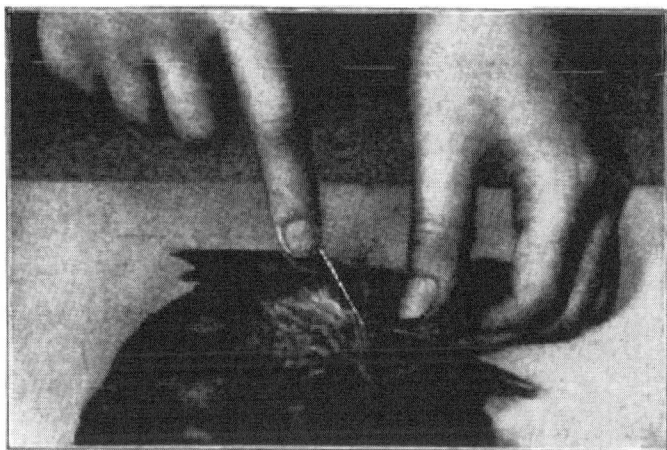

FIG. 74

QUILLS

82. Quills are very extensively used for trimming tailored hats for women and cheaper hats for schoolgirls. A quill is a single feather taken from either the end of the wing or the tail of a bird. The one shown in Fig. 75 is taken from a white goose wing. The quill may be sewed to a hat but it is much more effective if the lower end is stuck into the body of the hat, particularly if it is a straw, felt, or solid foundation. An effective position can be obtained by sticking a quill into the foundation that cannot be obtained by sewing it to the hat. A single feather used in this manner is known as a quill trimming.

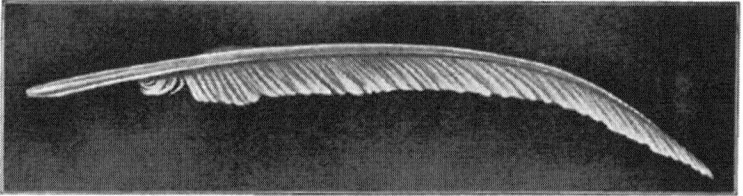

FIG. 75

83. The argus quill, shown in Fig. 76, is the most elaborate and possibly the most expensive of all quills. It is a very long feather having shades of white, black, and twc shades of brown in it, and is mottled with oval designs in golden brown, which

makes it a very handsome garniture for tailored or street hats. It varies from 12 to 48 in. in length and is usually long enough to encircle the crown, and have the end extend in the air at one side. It is a particularly effective trimming if used on tan, sand, or various shades of brown. All quills should be steamed, in order to straighten out the flues, before being placed on the hat.

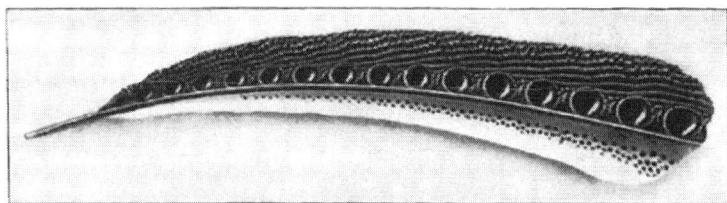

FIG. 76

84. The tetrus quill is a very wide quill having a soft velvety finish. Quills from the eagle, condor, turkey, goose, and numerous other birds are frequently used. The tail feather of the domesticated pheasant raised in this country is also used as a quill trimming for hats. This feather ranges in length from 3 to 6 ft. The United States government has excluded about seventy varieties of feathers from being imported to this country; consequently, the number of quills on the market is somewhat limited.

85. Feathered Pompon.—The feathered pompon shown in Fig. 77 is made of bunches of hackle feathers fastened tightly together at the bottom and then spread apart in order to make a rounded cluster. Feathers of this sort can be used for encircling the crowns of hats, and they may also be used at the base of quills, imitation aigrettes, wings, or any feathers that stand erect in the air. They are also used for trimming bonnets for elderly women where the trimming is to be low and flat. As they are tied together with wire they do not come apart easily.

FIG. 77

86. Imitation Aigrette.—The imitation aigrette shown in
Fig. 78 is made of feathers taken from a barnyard fowl and
soaked in acid to burn out part of the flues. They are then
curled with a curling knife in order to imitate paradise plumes.
The feathers at the bottom of the aigrette are made of hackle
feathers; consequently, the imitation aigrette can be worn in
any part of the world and is exceptionally good for trimming
small hats or bonnets for elderly women. Should the feathers
lose their curl from dampness they may be recurled by the use
of the curling knife.

FIG. 78

87. Ostaigrette.—An imitation of a heron's aigrette, made of ostrich feathers, and known as *ostaigrette*, is illustrated in Fig. 79. It is one of the cleverest imitations on the market and can be worn in any part of the world. It is very light in weight and is particularly good if used in connection with ostrich-feather trimming such as bands and small feathers that are made of the curled flues of the ostrich plume. This aigrette is particularly well adapted as a garniture for turbans and small, close-fitting shapes. It may also be used on wide-brimmed lace or net hats.

FIG. 79

88. Owl's Head.—The owl's head, shown in Fig. 80, is man-made and is constructed of white goose feathers fastened to a buckram foundation, the eyes and bill being made of small pieces of metal pressed into the proper form and then painted with black lacquer. Owls' heads are exceptionally good for trimming sport hats and hats for young ladies, particularly those worn during the months from May to August.

FIG. 80

89. Paradise Aigrette.—The paradise aigrette, shown in Fig. 81, is made of genuine paradise plumes taken from the male bird of paradise of New Guinea. It is one of the most expensive and elegant types of feather trimming used in millinery. Plumes of this kind cost from $15 to $50 according to the number of feathers in the cluster. The one shown in the illustration consists of several branching feathers held on silk-covered wires and spread in what is known as the fountain arrangement. Paradise plumes in the natural state take the form of a wing, and the long uncurled ends of the feather are generally allowed to fall over the edge of the hat. The natural colors of this feather are yellow or cedar brown. The paradise plume dyed black is extensively used for lace, net, fine velvet, or very elaborate dress hats, and the same can be said of the natural plume. They should not be used on heavy, coarse, straw-braid hats, nor, in fact, on any hat that is cheap in its make-up or construction.

FIG. 81

90. Goura.—The aigrette shown in Fig. 82 is a genuine goura, which comes from the top of the head of a very large pigeon found in Australia. As only a limited number of the feathers grow on each bird, they are very expensive, and should be classed with paradise plumes. They are quite light in weight and should be used only on expensive hats or bonnets for the elderly woman. Individual goura feathers may be used for edging wings and other fancy feather ornaments, but they are usually combined with other feathers that are used as a base for the goura aigrette. In the natural colors they are a dull stone gray, with white tips, but they can be dyed any color.

FIG. 82

91. Imitation Head of Bird of Paradise.—The imitation heads of the bird of paradise shown in Fig. 83 are made with celluloid beaks and the head and throat of each is made of velvet finished with chenille. They may have yellow tops and green throats, or they may be all black. One dozen of the imitation heads do not cost any more than one of the genuine. These heads are exceptionally clever if attached to the side crown of a hat so as to appear as though the bird were nesting inside the crown with only the head protruding. Two to four heads are generally used on one hat.

FIG. 83

92. Fancy Feather Made of Peacock Feathers.—The feather ornament shown in Fig. 84 is a fancy feather made of peacock feathers that have been dyed black, trimmed to the form shown, and painted white at the top to imitate coarse goura feathers. Feathers of this sort are particularly well adapted for trimming hats for mature women. They can also be used on lace, net, or hats made of light-weight transparent materials for younger women. As they are very light in weight, they should be used on hats that are daintily constructed.

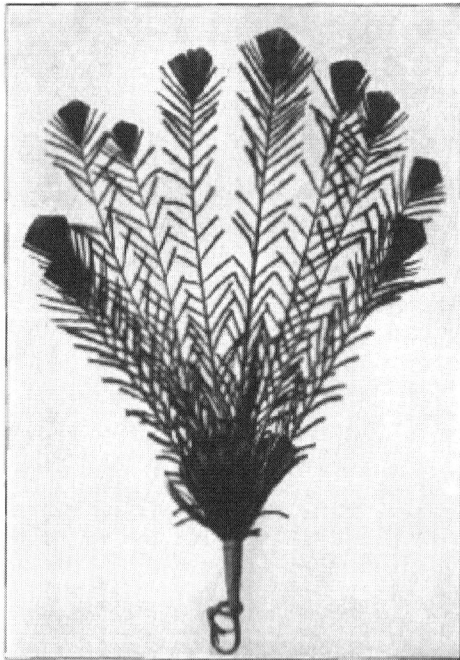

FIG. 84

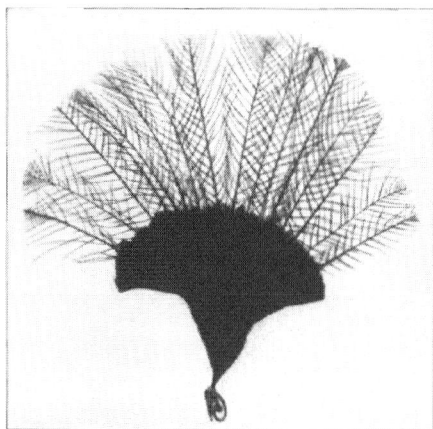

FIG. 85

FIG. 86

93. Fan Feather in Imitation of Goura.—The feather shown in Fig. 85 is very cheap because it can be made from goose feathers or any other inexpensive feather from which part of the flues can be burned away by acid. Feathers of this sort are particularly well adapted for being attached to the top of the crown, or used on the side crown so as to encircle the hat with the fan portion of the feather standing out from the side crown over the brim. As feathers of this kind are glued together and are more or less frail, they should always be placed on the hat so that they will be protected; in other words, they will last longer if they protected by the brim, so that the flues cannot be broken off easily.

94. Merle Bird.—The merle bird, shown in Fig. 86, is a small bird of very brilliant plumage. Its importation into this country is not restricted and it is used as a garniture for winter hats and also in connection with flowers and foliage for trimming summer hats. It is very light in weight. The same bird soaked in acid becomes a beautiful golden brown in color, known as the merle bird degradé.

FLOWERS AND FEATHERS

EXAMINATION QUESTIONS

(1)(*a*) How should cowslips be arranged as trimming? (*b*) How may butterflies be attached so as to appear to be fluttering over the flowers?

(2)(*a*) By whom may forget-me-nots be appropriately worn? (*b*) How are they arranged on a hat? (*c*) For whom are daisies most appropriate?

(3)(*a*) What is meant by a quill? (*b*) On what kinds of hats are quills used extensively?

(4)(*a*) Describe the Prince of Wales feathers. (*b*) For whose hats are they used? (*c*) How are they arranged and attached?

(5)(*a*) During what season of the year are violets particularly appropriate as a garniture? (*b*) If a hat is covered solidly with violets, how should it be trimmed?

(6)State the particular conditions under which the following flowers should be used: (*a*) Poinsettia; (*b*) orchid; (*c*) dogwood.

(7)Describe how currants may be used as a garniture on a

very firm wire foundation arranged like an arbor.

(8)(*a*) How may the vivid coloring of dandelions be toned down? (*b*) On what kinds of hats may they be used to advantage?

(9)(*a*) What is an ostaigrette? (*b*) On what kinds of hats are ostaigrettes used?

(10)How should natural wings be treated to protect them from the attacks of moths?

(11)(*a*) How may the stem of an ostrich feather be bent to a desired form? (*b*) What is a lobster feather? (*c*) What is an Amazon plume?

(12)(*a*) To whom does the pansy belong, as a trimming? (*b*) By whom should dark blue and purple pansies be worn? (*c*) Under what conditions may pansies be used on children's hats?

(13)Why are artificial flowers made of muslin preferable to those made of silk?

(14)(*a*) Why should silk crab apples be used sparingly on a hat? (*b*) On what kinds of hats should they be placed?

(15)(*a*) For what type of woman is the fuchsia trimming adapted? (*b*) Why? (*c*) How may the heavy appearance of fuchsia trimming be lightened?

(16)(*a*) What is the nature of Alsatian wings? (*b*) How may they be arranged on a hat?

(17) State the kinds of hats on which the following should be used: (*a*) Mistletoe; (*b*) aster foliage; (*c*) geranium foliage.

(18)(*a*) What is meant by man-made wings or birds? (*b*) Why are they an improvement over the natural kinds? (*c*) How may they be arranged on a hat?

(19)(*a*) How is natural wheat treated to make it available as a trimming for hats? (*b*) With what kinds of field flowers should it be used?

(20)(*a*) What type of woman should avoid poppies as trimmings? (*b*) With what type are they particularly becoming?

21770183R00097

Printed in Great Britain
by Amazon